OUR COMMUNITY™

Let's Visit the Bank

Marianne Johnston

The Rosen Publishing Group's
PowerKids Press™
New York

Published in 2000 by The Rosen Publishing Group, Inc.
29 East 21st Street, New York, NY 10010

First Edition

Book Design: Danielle Primiceri

Photo Credits: Cover © Horii/International Stock; p. 4 © John Michael/International Stock; p. 7 © North Wind Pictures; p. 8 © Michael Krasowitz/FPG International; p. 11 © Steve Smith/FPG International; pp. 12 © Jim Cummins/FPG International, James Davis/International Stock, Patrick Ramsey/International Stock; p. 15, 16 by Bonnie Rotstein-Brewer; p. 19 © Patrick Ramsey/International Stock; p. 20 © Jim Cummins/FPG International.

Johnston, Marianne
    Let's visit the bank / by Marianne Johnston.
       p.   cm. — (Our community)
    Summary: Explains what banks are, the activities they perform, and the role they play in the community
    ISBN 0-8239-5432-3 (lib. bdg.)
    1. Banks and banking Juvenile literature.   [1. Banks and banking.]   I. Title. II. Series:
Johnston, Marianne. Our community.
HG1609.J64   1999
332.1'0973—dc21   99-19102
                                                              CIP

Manufactured in the United States of America

Contents

Why Do We Need Banks?

When you pass by a bank, do you think of stacks of money sitting in a giant steel vault? Banks do a lot more for the people of your **community** than just give them a safe way to save money. Banks help keep the community running smoothly.

The people who run the store down the street probably borrowed money from a bank to help them get started. In fact, it is very likely that a bank even helped your parents buy the house you live in or the car they drive.

◀ *Today, almost every community has a bank.*

The History of Banks

A long time ago, people didn't use money. Instead, they traded things of value, such as flour or milk, for something else of equal value, like eggs or sugar. About 2,500 years ago, people began to use coins. Coins were much smaller than bartering items, so people could carry them around. That way they always had something to trade if they saw something they wanted. The ancient Greeks stored their coins in temples that served as simple banks. Close to 600 years ago, bigger and more complex banks started appearing.

Stores like this one, called the Hudson Bay Company, traded goods instead of money for their products. ▶

Today's Banks

Today, there are lots of different banks. Banks are run by big companies. The bank you see in your community is a branch of the banking company. These days, almost everyone uses a bank in some way.

Lots of people keep their money in a bank by putting it into an **account**. Having an account at the bank allows you to keep money with the bank. An account also helps you keep track of how much money you have and how often you add money or take money out of the bank.

◄ *People often need help from the bank to get started.*

9

The Teller

The people you see behind the long counters at the bank are called tellers. They help customers make deposits or withdrawals, which means adding money into or taking money out of an account.

Each time someone changes the amount of money in her account, the teller must record it on the bank's computer. Then he gives the customer a **receipt**. The customer keeps this receipt to remind her of how much money she put in or took out of this account.

Tellers must be good with numbers to deal with all that money. ▷

Other People at the Bank

When you walk into your bank, you may notice several people sitting at desks in the lobby. These people are customer service representatives. They help you start checking accounts and **savings accounts**. They also answer any questions you might have about your account.

Another very important job at the bank is that of the **loan** officers. They are the people you talk to if you want to borrow money.

The branch manager keeps track of all the tellers and the customer service people.

People who want a loan for their business need to talk to the commercial loan officer.

How Loans Work

Banks loan people in your community money. When a person gets a loan from a bank, the person promises to pay the bank back a little bit at a time. In return, he needs to offer the bank **collateral**, or something of value the bank can take if the person doesn't pay it back. The bank will only loan someone money if the person has enough collateral.

Loans allow people to buy things they really need but can't afford, by letting them pay over a long period of time instead of all at once.

People sometimes need loans to buy large objects, such as cars or houses. ▶

How Banks Make Money

In order to keep being able to loan people money and provide services for people in the community, the bank must make money, too. Banks do that by charging **interest** on their loans. This means that when you borrow money from the bank, you have to pay it all back, plus some extra. For instance, if you borrow 100 dollars, you might have to pay 110 dollars back to the bank. Another way banks make money is by charging customers **fees**. Fees are small amounts of money that banks charge for certain services.

◀ *This mother and son pay their bills with checks from their checking account.*

Technology at the Bank

Before computers existed, bank workers had to write everything down about someone's account in a book. Now banks use computers to keep track of all the accounts. Some banks even have a phone number that you can call to open an account from home.

Many banks now also have **automatic teller machines**, or ATMs. These machines do what tellers do inside the bank. A person can make a withdrawal or a deposit using the machine. This makes it easier for people to get money if they are in a hurry or if the bank is closed.

Many people use ATMs to withdraw money from or deposit money into their bank accounts. ▶

Starting Your Own Bank Account

Do you get money for your birthday each year? Do you earn an allowance? If you do, then you should think about asking your parents to help you open a savings account at the bank. The money in your savings account acts like a loan that you make to the bank, so the bank pays you interest on that money.

When you get to the bank, go to a customer service representative. She will take the money you want to use to start your account.

This girl is using all the money in her piggy bank to start a savings account.

The Future of Banks

As people do more of their banking over the computer, banks will need fewer tellers and more computers. Though banks are changing, our need for them isn't. Whether we go to the bank in person or over the computer, banks are an important part of keeping our communities running smoothly.

Web Sites:

You can learn more about banking on the Internet. Check out this Web site: http://www.moneykids.com

Glossary

account (ah-KOWNT) A way to store money and keep a record of it.

automatic teller machines (aw-toh-MA-tik TE-ler mah-SHEENZ) Machines that do what the tellers do; you can use these machines to make withdrawals or deposits.

collateral (koh-LAT-er-ul) Something the bank can take if you don't pay back the money they loaned you.

community (kuh-MYOO-nih-tee) A group of people who have something in common, such as a special interest or the area where they live.

fees (FEEZ) The small amounts of money the bank makes customers pay for doing certain things for them.

interest (IN-ter-est) The extra money that you pay to the bank when you pay back a loan.

loan (LOHN) The money a bank gives to a person that the person pays back a little bit at a time.

receipt (reh-SEET) The slip of paper the teller gives you showing how much money you put into or took out of your account.

savings account (SAY-vingz ah-KOWNT) The money you put into a bank for safekeeping.

Index